Renewed

The Transformational Power
of Putting Off the Old and
Putting On the New

© 2024 Alisa L. Grace

All rights reserved.

No part of this book may be reproduced in any form or by any electronic or mechanical means, including information storage and retrieval systems, without permission in writing from the publisher.

Self-Published by

Alisa L. Grace

Sanford, FL 32771

ISBN: 9781966129448

First Edition

Printed in the United States of America

Library of Congress Cataloging-in-Publication Data

Grace, Alisa L.

Title of the Book: Renewed: The Transformational Power of Putting off the Old and Putting on the New

Library of Congress Control Number: 2024925237

Disclaimer: The views expressed in this book are those of the author and do not necessarily reflect any organizations or individuals mentioned.

Acknowledgments: The author wishes to thank God, Her Husband (Linion), Victory Temple of God, Florida SPECS, Unity Youth Association, All About Serving You, Angels-ANJ Events, NordeVest, and Love & Create Life for their support and contributions.

Dedication

To everyone who desires a life fully pleasing to God, walking in alignment with His design and reflecting His character. May this book guide you in the transformation journey, leading you closer to the life He created for you. May your heart be open to His work, and may you be renewed, restored, and empowered to live as a true reflection of Christ.

Determination Survey

Before you embark on this journey, take a few moments to reflect on your spiritual walk and your desire for transformation. This survey will help you determine your readiness to let go of the old and embrace the new.

1. Are you willing to let go of attitudes and habits that hinder your walk with God?

- Yes
- No
- Not Sure

2. Do you desire to cultivate godly virtues that align with God's heart?

- Yes
- No
- Maybe

3. How would you describe your current spiritual journey?

- Growing steadily

- Stagnant and uncertain
- Struggling or distant

4. Are you committed to seeking genuine transformation, even when challenging?

- Yes
- No
- Unsure

5. What is one area of your life where you most desire God's transformative power?

(Write your answer here)

_____
_____
_____
_____
_____
_____
_____
_____
_____
_____
_____

Welcome Letter

Dear Friend,

I'm so glad you're holding this book, and I want to welcome you to a life-changing journey. This journey isn't just about making lifestyle adjustments or changing certain behaviors; it's about experiencing a complete heart transformation. This book is for those who desire a life that reflects God's love, wisdom, and strength.

Each chapter will invite you to "put off" what separates you from God and "put on" the virtues that allow you to grow closer to Him. You'll find stories, reflection questions, and powerful truths that encourage you to look deeply into your heart and embrace the life God has for you.

May this journey bless you, draw you closer to God, and bring you to a place of renewal and joy as you walk in alignment with His will.

With love in Christ,
Your Sister In Christ

Why Read This Book?

If you're ready for profound transformation and desire to grow closer to God, this book is for you. This isn't about quick fixes or surface-level change; it's a journey toward true heart transformation that aligns you with God's purpose.

In this book, you will learn:

- The behaviors and attitudes God calls us to "put off."

- The virtues God desires us to "put on."

- How to experience true transformation and live as a new creation in Christ.

- Practical steps for living out a Christ-centered life each day.

Each section includes stories, examples, and reflection questions to help you explore these truths deeply. With an open heart and a willing spirit, you'll find a transformation that leads you closer to God and His purpose for your life.

Contents

Introduction   9

Section 1: Clearing the Path to Peace: Putting Off What God Hates   10

Section 2: Clothing Yourself in Christ: Embracing the Virtues God Loves   17

Section 3: Becoming New: Embracing Your Identity in Christ   24

Section 4: Living the Transformation: Practical Steps to Walk in Renewal   36

Conclusion   41

30 Days to Renewed: Embracing God's Transformation   44

Days 1-7: Clearing the Path to Peace   46

Days 8-16: Clothing Yourself in Christ   55

Days 17-23: Becoming a New Creature   66

Days 24-30: Living the Transformation   75

Additional Resources   85

Meet the Author: Alisa Ladawn Grace   90

Introduction

We all desire a life that reflects our faith, filled with purpose, peace, and a deep connection with God. Yet, we often hold onto behaviors, attitudes, and mindsets that distance us from the life He intended for us. This book is about letting go of those things, "putting off" what hinders us, and "putting on" the qualities that draw us closer to God.

In Proverbs 6:16-19, the Bible lists behaviors God hates, including pride, lying, and stirring up conflict. These are not just sinful actions; they reflect deeper attitudes that can block us from fully experiencing God's presence. But in His love, God offers a way to transform. Through Christ, we can "put off" these harmful behaviors and "put on" virtues like humility, compassion, and love, becoming more like Christ and living in peace and purpose.

Each chapter of this book will help you release what holds you back and embrace godly qualities that lead to a fulfilling, transformed life. I hope that you will approach each section with an open heart, ready to become renewed in Christ.

Your Transformation Starts Now!

Section 1:
Clearing the Path to Peace: Putting Off What God Hates

In this section, we'll explore the behaviors and attitudes that Proverbs 6:16-19 describes as detestable to God. These harmful traits—such as pride, dishonesty, anger, and divisiveness—clutter our hearts and block the light of God's presence and peace. Just as clutter in a home prevents us from enjoying it thoroughly, these attitudes hinder us from experiencing the fullness of God's love. Letting go of these attitudes clears the path to a renewed and peaceful relationship with God.

Scripture Support:

> "There are six things the Lord hates, seven that are detestable to him: haughty eyes, a lying tongue, hands that shed innocent blood, a heart that devises wicked schemes, feet that are quick to rush into evil, a false witness who pours out lies, and a person who stirs up conflict in the community." — **Proverbs 6:16-19**

> "Rid yourselves of all such things as these: anger, rage, malice, slander, and filthy language from your lips." — **Colossians 3:8**

What You Will Learn:

- Why do these behaviors block your spiritual growth and peace.

- How to recognize and release these attitudes from your life.

- The impact of letting go of these behaviors on your relationship with God.

Clearing Out the Clutter

This story explores the idea of our hearts becoming cluttered with harmful attitudes and behaviors that block the light of God's presence. Like a cluttered home, our hearts need to be cleared of the pride, anger, and deceit that weigh us down and keep us from experiencing God's peace.

Imagine a home filled with clutter and dirt. Over time, once valuable items became unnecessary, but instead of being removed, they were piled up, blocking doorways and filling every corner. Dust and grime accumulated, making the space dark, unwelcoming, and unhealthy. Our hearts can become like this home when we hold onto attitudes such as pride, deceit, and anger. These "cluttered" attitudes prevent God's light from entering our lives, weighing down our spirits and keeping us from the joy He offers. In this section, you'll begin clearing the clutter, allowing God's peace and presence to fill your heart.

The Behaviors in Proverbs 6:16-19 and Their Dangers

1. **Haughty Eyes (Pride)**

   Definition: Pride and arrogance, looking down on others.

   Danger: Pride distances us from God, breaks down relationships, and closes our eyes to our own flaws.

   Scripture: "The Lord detests all the proud of heart" (Proverbs 16:5).

2. **A Lying Tongue (Dishonesty and Deceit)**

   Definition: Speaking falsehoods or misleading others.

   Danger: Dishonesty destroys trust, creates confusion, and leads to a life of deceit.

   Scripture: "Do not lie to each other" (Colossians 3:9).

3. **Hands that Shed Innocent Blood (Violence)**

   Definition: Harmful actions toward innocent people.

   Danger: Violence disregards the sanctity of life, leads to a cycle of harm, and desensitizes the heart.

   Scripture: "You shall not murder" (Exodus 20:13).

4. **A Heart that Devises Wicked Schemes (Evil Intentions)**

Definition: Plotting harm or injustice against others.

Danger: Evil intentions corrupt our hearts and foster an environment of mistrust and fear.

Scripture: "The devising of folly is sin" (Proverbs 24:9).

5. **Feet that are Quick to Rush into Evil (Impulsiveness toward Sin)**

    Definition: Readiness to engage in wrongdoing.

    Danger: Quickness to sin creates harmful habits, influences others negatively, and blocks moral restraint.

    Scripture: "Do not set foot on the path of the wicked" (Proverbs 4:14).

6. **A False Witness Who Pours Out Lies (Perjury and Slander)**

    Definition: Spreading falsehoods, especially in legal matters.

    Danger: Slander destroys reputations, undermines justice, and divides communities.

    Scripture: "You shall not give false testimony" (Exodus 20:16).

7. **A Person Who Stirs Up Conflict (Discord)**

    Definition: Creating division among people.

    Danger: Stirring conflict fractures unity, creates hostility, and encourages division.

Scripture: "Blessed are the peacemakers" (Matthew 5:9).

Transformational Questions:

1. What "clutter" in your heart prevents you from experiencing God's peace?

   _____
   _____
   _____
   _____

2. Are there attitudes you hold onto that damage your relationships with others?

   _____
   _____
   _____
   _____

3. How willing are you to release these behaviors, knowing they keep you from growing spiritually?

   _____
   _____
   _____
   _____

Section 2:
Clothing Yourself in Christ: Embracing the Virtues God Loves

This section focuses on the godly virtues that God calls us to "put on," as described in Colossians 3:12-14. Like a treasured garment, compassion, kindness, humility, gentleness, patience, forgiveness, and love clothe us in Christ's character, allowing us to reflect His love to others. These virtues are essential for our growth and fostering unity and harmony in our relationships. Embracing these qualities brings us closer to God and allows His light to shine through us.

Scripture Support:

- "Therefore, as God's chosen people, holy and dearly loved, clothe yourselves with compassion, kindness, humility, gentleness, and patience. Bear with each other and forgive one another... And over all these virtues put on love, which binds them all together in perfect unity." — **Colossians 3:12-14**

- "But the fruit of the Spirit is love, joy, peace, forbearance, kindness, goodness, faithfulness, gentleness, and self-control." — **Galatians 5:22-23**

What You Will Learn:

- The essential qualities that reflect God's character.

  _____
  _____
  _____
  _____

- How these virtues will bring you closer to God and enrich your relationships.

  _____
  _____
  _____
  _____

- Practical steps to "put on" these Christ-like qualities in your daily life.

  _____
  _____
  _____
  _____

Wearing the Coat of Virtue

This story likens godly virtues to a treasured coat passed down through generations, offering warmth, protection, and identity. We are clothed in Christ's strength and peace whenever we "put on" qualities like kindness, compassion, and love. Embracing these virtues helps us live as reflections of His love.

Picture a treasured winter coat passed down through generations. When a family member wears it, they feel warmth, protection, and a sense of connection to their heritage. In the same way, when we "put on" the virtues of Christ, we are wrapped in His love, strength, and peace. These virtues protect our hearts and allow us to navigate life gracefully and confidently. In this section, you'll learn how to clothe yourself in these godly qualities, bringing warmth to your spirit and strength to your relationships.

The Godly Virtues and Their Importance

1. **Compassion**

    Definition: Deep sympathy for others, coupled with a desire to help.

    Importance: Compassion builds empathy and strengthens relationships.

    Scripture: "Clothe yourselves with compassion" (Colossians 3:12).

2. **Kindness**

    Definition: Acting with generosity and consideration toward others.

    Importance: Kindness builds trust and encourages unity.

    Scripture: "Be kind and compassionate" (Ephesians 4:32).

3. **Humility**

    Definition: Valuing others above yourself and recognizing dependence on God.

    Importance: Humility allows for growth and strengthens relationships.

    Scripture: "In humility value others above yourselves" (Philippians 2:3).

4. **Gentleness**

   Definition: Strength under control, shown through patience and kindness.

   Importance: Gentleness fosters trust and de-escalates conflict.

   Scripture: "Let your gentleness be evident to all" (Philippians 4:5).

5. **Patience**

   Definition: Enduring trials and difficulties without anger.

   Importance: Patience brings peace and prevents conflicts.

   Scripture: "Be patient, bearing with one another" (Ephesians 4:2).

6. **Love**

   Definition: Selfless concern for others, seeking their highest good.

   Importance: Love unifies and reflects the heart of God.

   Scripture: "Over all these virtues put on love" (Colossians 3:14).

7. **Forgiveness**

    Definition: Letting go of resentment and offering pardon.

    Importance: Forgiveness restores relationships and promotes healing.

    Scripture: "Forgive as the Lord forgave you" (Colossians 3:13).

Transformational Questions:

1. Which virtues do you most desire to put on in your life?

   _____
   _____
   _____
   _____

2. How would embracing these virtues transform your relationships and experiences?

   _____
   _____
   _____
   _____

3. What steps can you take to develop qualities like compassion, kindness, and love?

   _____
   _____
   _____
   _____

Section 3:
Becoming New: Embracing Your Identity in Christ

Transformation in Christ means leaving behind our old ways and embracing a new identity rooted in God's love. This section guides you in putting off the old self and stepping into the life of a new creation, as described in 2 Corinthians 5:17. Being a new creation in Christ is not about simply improving ourselves but about fully embracing our God-given identity and walking in the freedom, joy, and purpose He designed for us. This renewal draws us closer to God, empowering us to live as His children, loved and accepted.

Scripture Support:

> "Therefore, if anyone is in Christ, the new creation has come: The old has gone, the new is here!" — **2 Corinthians 5:17**

> "You were taught, with regard to your former way of life, to put off your old self, which is being corrupted by its deceitful desires... and to put on the new self, created to be like God in true righteousness and holiness." — **Ephesians 4:22-24**

What You Will Learn:

- The true meaning of becoming a new creation in Christ.
- How to release old habits and mindsets.
- The power of living in your new identity in Christ.

Breaking Free and Taking Flight

This story uses the metaphor of a butterfly emerging from its cocoon to illustrate the transformation of becoming a new creature in Christ. Leaving behind our old nature, we take flight into a life of freedom and purpose, stepping into the beautiful, renewed identity that God has given us.

Imagine a butterfly emerging from its cocoon. Once confined, it now takes flight, transformed and free. Like the butterfly, you are called to leave behind the things that confine you and step into the beautiful, free life God designed for you. This section will guide you through this transformation, helping you experience the freedom and purpose of being a new creature in Christ.

The Meaning of Putting Off the Old Self and Putting On the New

Putting Off the Old Self: Letting go of sinful behaviors, attitudes, and desires that no longer define you.

Impact: Releases burdens and clears the way for growth.

Putting On the New Self: Embracing a Christ-centered life rooted in God's love, purpose, and character.

Impact: Brings joy, freedom, and deeper intimacy with God.

The Meaning of Putting Off the Old Self and Putting On the New

The Bible calls us to a life of transformation, not simply by changing our outward behaviors but by renewing our entire being—mind, heart, and spirit. Central to this transformation is the command to "put off the old self" and "put on the new self," a process that reshapes us into the image of Christ and aligns our lives with God's will. This chapter explores what this means, why it matters, and how it transforms us.

The Meaning of Putting Off the Old Self and Putting On the New

Transformation in Christ is not just about modifying behavior or striving to be a "better person." It's a complete renewal of our identity, rooted in God's love and empowered by His Spirit. The Bible calls this process **putting off the old self** and **putting on the new self.** To fully embrace this transformation, we must understand what it means to leave behind the old and embrace the new.

Putting Off the Old Self

Definition:

Putting off the old self means letting go of sinful behaviors, attitudes, and desires that are part of our fallen nature. These are the traits we exhibited before knowing Christ—pride, anger, deceit, greed, and selfishness—that reflect our separation from God.

Paul writes in Ephesians 4:22-24, "You were taught, with regard to your former way of life, to put off your old self, which is being corrupted by its deceitful desires; to be made new in the attitude of your minds; and to put on the new self, created to be like God in true righteousness and holiness." This passage emphasizes the intentional decision to let go of anything that corrupts or distances us from God.

What the Old Self Looks Like:

Sinful Behaviors: These include actions like lying, stealing, gossiping, and sexual immorality.

- *Scripture:* "Do not lie to each other, since you have taken off your old self with its practices." — **Colossians 3:9**

Destructive Attitudes: Pride, bitterness, envy, and anger are traits of the old self.

- *Scripture:* "Get rid of all bitterness, rage and anger, brawling and slander, along with every form of malice." — **Ephesians 4:31**

Self-Centered Desires: Seeking personal gratification, power, or material possessions above all else.

- *Scripture:* "Put to death, therefore, whatever belongs to your earthly nature: sexual immorality, impurity, lust, evil desires, and greed, which is idolatry." — **Colossians 3:5**

Why It's Essential to Put Off the Old Self:

The old self represents our life before Christ—a life enslaved to sin and separated from God. Holding onto these traits:

Prevents Growth: Sin blocks our ability to grow spiritually and keeps us stagnant in our faith.

Weighs Us Down: These behaviors and attitudes are burdensome, leaving us feeling guilty, ashamed, or unfulfilled.

Separates Us from God: The old self reflects a nature that is incompatible with God's holiness.

- *Scripture:* "For the wages of sin is death, but the gift of God is eternal life in Christ Jesus our Lord." — **Romans 6:23**

Impact of Letting Go:

When we put off the old self, we release the burdens that weigh us down and make room for God's transformative work in our lives. This process clears the path for spiritual growth and renewed intimacy with God.

Putting On the New Self

Definition:

Putting on the new self is about fully embracing the identity God has given us as His children. It means adopting Christ-like virtues—

compassion, kindness, humility, patience, and love—and living a life centered on God's purpose.

Paul writes in Colossians 3:10, "...and have put on the new self, which is being renewed in knowledge in the image of its Creator." This emphasizes that the new self reflects God's image and aligns with His design for our lives.

What the New Self Looks Like:

Christ-Like Virtues: These include qualities such as compassion, humility, forgiveness, and love.

- *Scripture:* "Therefore, as God's chosen people, holy and dearly loved, clothe yourselves with compassion, kindness, humility, gentleness and patience." — **Colossians 3:12**

Renewed Mind: Thinking in alignment with God's truth and focusing on what is noble, pure, and praiseworthy.

- *Scripture:* "Do not conform to the pattern of this world, but be transformed by the renewing of your mind." — **Romans 12:2**

Purpose-Driven Life: Living in a way that glorifies God and fulfills His purpose for us.

- *Scripture:* "For we are God's handiwork, created in Christ Jesus to do good works, which God prepared in advance for us to do." — **Ephesians 2:10**

Why It's Essential to Put On the New Self:

The new self reflects our new identity in Christ—a life reconciled to God and empowered by His Spirit. Embracing the new self:

- **Brings Joy and Freedom:** We are no longer bound by sin but free to live in God's love and grace.

- **Fosters Intimacy with God:** Living in alignment with God's will deepens our relationship with Him.

- **Reflects God's Image:** Our lives testify to His transformative power to the world.

Impact of Putting On the New Self:

Putting on the new self allows us to experience the fullness of life in Christ. It brings joy, freedom, and purpose as we walk in deeper intimacy with God and reflect His love to others.

How to Transition from the Old Self to the New Self

1. **Acknowledge Your Need for Change:** Recognize the areas where the old self is still present.

- *Prayer Prompt:* "Lord, show me the areas in my life where I need to let go of old habits or attitudes that don't honor You."

2. **Surrender to God:** Fully submit your heart and desires to Him, trusting Him to do the work of transformation.

- *Scripture:* "Submit yourselves, then, to God. Resist the devil, and he will flee from you." — **James 4:7**

Daily Renewal: Spend time in God's Word and prayer to renew your mind and strengthen your resolve to live as a new creation.

- *Scripture:* "Your word is a lamp for my feet, a light on my path." — **Psalm 119:105**

Practice Christ-Like Virtues: Consciously choose to act in love, kindness, humility, and patience, even when it's complicated.

- *Example:* When someone wrongs you, choose forgiveness over resentment.

Surround Yourself with Support: Connect with a community of believers who will encourage and hold you accountable.

- *Scripture:* "As iron sharpens iron, so one person sharpens another." — **Proverbs 27:17**

Encouragement for the Journey

The journey of putting off the old self and putting on the new is not always easy, but it is deeply rewarding. As you let go of the burdens of the past and embrace the freedom of living in Christ, you will experience the transformation that touches every part of your life. God has created you for a purpose, and as you step into your new identity, you will reflect His love and grace to the world.

Remember, this process is not about perfection but about daily progress. God's Spirit is with you, empowering you to live as a new creation and guiding you to become who He designed you to be. Keep moving forward in faith, trusting that His grace is sufficient for every step of this journey.

Transformational Questions:

1. What habits or mindsets must you let go of to experience transformation fully?

   _____
   _____
   _____
   _____

2. How does becoming a new creation in Christ inspire you to live differently?

   _____
   _____
   _____
   _____

3. What steps can you take to renew your mind and embrace your God-given identity?

   _____
   _____
   _____
   _____

Section 4:
Living the Transformation: Practical Steps to Walk in Renewal

This final section provides practical tools and daily steps to live out the transformation God has begun in you. Through intentional habits like daily reflection, prayer, Scripture meditation, and seeking accountability, you can sustain your journey of renewal and continually align your heart with God's will. These practices and specific examples from Scripture help you stay committed to "putting on" the virtues of Christ and shedding the behaviors of the old self. Transformation is an ongoing process; with each step, you grow closer to God and become more like Christ.

Scripture Support:

> "Do not conform to the pattern of this world, but be transformed by the renewing of your mind. Then you will be able to test and approve what God's will is—his good, pleasing and perfect will." — **Romans 12:2**

> "For physical training is of some value, but godliness has value for all things, holding promise for both the present life and the life to come." — **1 Timothy 4:8**

What You Will Learn:

- How to make lasting changes in your life.

- Practical ways to embody Christ-like virtues daily.

- Tools to sustain your transformation journey with God.

Training for the Race of Faith

In this story, the journey of transformation is compared to a runner training for a marathon. Just as a runner builds endurance and strength step by step, we also grow in faith by actively choosing to "put off" old habits and "put on" godly virtues. Each daily choice strengthens us to live a life that honors God and finishes the race well.

Think of a runner training for a marathon. They can't reach the finish line by merely wishing for it; they need to train step by step, building strength and endurance. Just like the runner, you'll learn how to practice "putting off" what holds you back and "putting on" the virtues that will allow you to run the race of faith strong. This section will help you turn the insights of this book into daily habits that align you with God's will.

Practical Steps to Putting Off and Putting On

1. **Daily Reflection:** Set aside time each day to reflect on areas where you need to "put off" and "put on."

2. **Seek God's Strength in Prayer:** Pray for God's guidance to release old habits and cultivate godly virtues.

3. **Scripture Meditation:** Meditate on verses that speak to the virtues you wish to develop.

4. **Actively Practice:** Identify small, daily ways to "put on" virtues like kindness, patience, and forgiveness.

5. **Seek Accountability:** Connect with a mentor or friend who will support you in your journey.

Transformational Questions:

1. What daily habits can you start to help you "put off" old behaviors?

   _____
   _____
   _____
   _____

2. Which Christ-like virtue will you focus on practicing this week?

   _____
   _____
   _____
   _____

3. How can you ensure you stay committed to your journey of transformation?

   _____
   _____
   _____
   _____

Conclusion

As you reach the end of this book, I invite you to pause and reflect on each step of this journey and the transformation God desires for you. Each section has been a call to let go of what separates you from God and to embrace a life that reflects His love, purpose, and character.

In **Section 1**, you explored the behaviors and attitudes God hates—the "clutter" that keeps us from experiencing His peace. You recognized how pride, dishonesty, anger, and other harmful behaviors block the light of God's presence in your life. Releasing these isn't always easy, but remember that God doesn't ask us to do this alone. He provides strength and grace to help us let go of anything that hinders our walk with Him.

Call to Action: Take time to pray and ask God to reveal any lingering attitudes or habits you need to put off. Trust that He will guide you as you clear the path to experiencing His peace more fully.

In **Section 2**, you discovered the beautiful qualities God calls us to "put on"—the virtues of humility, compassion, kindness, patience, and love. These are not just qualities to admire; they are the building blocks of a life that reflects Christ. As you clothe yourself in these virtues, you embody God's love in a way that touches others and transforms your relationships.

Call to Action: Reflect on which virtues you feel God is calling you to cultivate more deeply. Pray for daily opportunities to "put on" these qualities, whether through a kind word, a patient response, or an act of compassion.

Section 3 invites you into the life of a new creation. To put off the old self and put on the new is to embrace your identity as a child of God, transformed by His love. In Christ, you are no longer defined by past mistakes, old habits, or fears—you are renewed and empowered to live in His freedom and purpose.

Call to Action: Take a moment to thank God for the new identity He's given you in Christ. If any past patterns try to pull you back, remind yourself of who you are—a new creation loved and accepted by God. Walk forward with confidence, knowing that your life is rooted in Him.

Finally, **Section 4** gave you practical tools and steps to live out this transformation each day. True change requires intentionality, commitment, and support. Putting off the old and putting on the new is a daily decision, but it is also a journey filled with grace and growth.

Call to Action: Choose one or two of the practical steps from this section that resonate with you. Make them a part of your daily life, whether it's through prayer, Scripture meditation, or seeking accountability. Trust that as you make these small, intentional steps, God will continue to shape and strengthen you.

A Final Encouragement

This journey doesn't end with the last page. Transformation is a continual process, a daily decision to live in alignment with God's will. Every day presents a new opportunity to put off what no longer serves you and to put on the qualities that bring you closer to Him. Remember, God is with you every step of the way, cheering you on, offering grace, and inviting you to deeper intimacy with Him.

I pray that you will continue to pursue this journey wholeheartedly, knowing that God's love for you is unchanging and His desire for your life is greater than you can imagine. Keep seeking His heart, growing in His love, and putting on the virtues that reflect His character. As you do, may you experience the fullness of life He designed for you—a life marked by peace, purpose, and profound joy in Christ.

Go forth with courage, and let your transformation be a light to others. May you be renewed, restored, and empowered to live the life God created you to live.

With love and encouragement,
Your Sister In Christ

30 Days to Renewed:
Embracing God's Transformation

Welcome Letter

Dear Friend,

Welcome to **"30 Days to Renewed: Embracing God's Transformation!"** I am so excited you've taken this step to begin a journey that can change your life from the inside out. This challenge isn't just a set of daily tasks; it's a powerful invitation to let go of what separates you from God and embrace the virtues that bring you closer to Him. Over the next 30 days, you'll be guided to "put off" behaviors and attitudes that weigh you down and "put on" the qualities that reflect the character of Christ.

Each day, you'll be encouraged with a scripture to ground you in God's truth and a reflective question to deepen your understanding. This journey calls for an open heart and a willing spirit—true transformation requires stepping outside of our comfort zones and allowing God to work in our lives. But remember, you're not alone. God is with you, and I am cheering you on every step of the way.

Some days may feel challenging, but know that each small step forward brings you closer to the life God designed for you—a life of purpose, peace, and joy. My prayer is that through this journey, you'll experience a renewed sense of God's presence and a closer connection to His love. Take it one day at a time, trusting that as you open your heart, God will meet, guide, and transform you in ways you may have never imagined.

Let's begin this journey with faith and anticipation, knowing God has beautiful things in store for you.

With love and encouragement,
Your Sister In Christ

Days 1-7:
Clearing the Path to Peace

(Letting Go of What God Hates)

Day 1: Let Go of Pride

Scripture: "Pride goes before destruction, a haughty spirit before a fall." — **Proverbs 16:18**

Reflection Question: Where has pride kept me from connecting with God and others? How can humility open new doors in my relationships?

_____
_____
_____
_____
_____
_____
_____
_____
_____
_____
_____
_____
_____
_____
_____
_____
_____
_____
_____
_____

Day 2: Release Dishonesty

Scripture: "The Lord detests lying lips, but he delights in people who are trustworthy." — **Proverbs 12:22**

Reflection Question: Is there an area where I need to be more honest with myself or others? How can truth bring freedom?

Day 3: Let Go of Anger

Scripture: "In your anger do not sin; do not let the sun go down while you are still angry." — **Ephesians 4:26**

Reflection Question: What past or present anger am I holding onto? How can releasing it open my heart to peace?

_____
_____
_____
_____
_____
_____
_____
_____
_____
_____
_____
_____
_____
_____
_____
_____
_____
_____
_____

Day 4: Turn Away from Wicked Thoughts

Scripture: "The Lord detests the thoughts of the wicked, but gracious words are pure in his sight." — **Proverbs 15:26**

Reflection Question: Are there negative or harmful thoughts I'm allowing to linger? How can I replace these thoughts with ones that honor God?

Day 5: Resist Rushing into Sin

Scripture: "Do not be quick with your mouth, do not be hasty in your heart to utter anything before God." — **Ecclesiastes 5:2**

Reflection Question: Where am I prone to rush into poor decisions? How can slowing down leads me to God's wisdom?

Day 6: Avoid Slander and False Speech

Scripture: "Do not spread false reports. Do not help a guilty person by being a malicious witness." — **Exodus 23:1**

Reflection Question: Are there times when I speak negatively about others? How can I use my words to build up rather than tear down?

_____
_____
_____
_____
_____
_____
_____
_____
_____
_____
_____
_____
_____
_____
_____
_____
_____
_____
_____

Day 7: Pursue Peace over Conflict

Scripture: "Make every effort to live in peace with everyone and to be holy." — **Hebrews 12:14**

Reflection Question: Where am I creating or sustaining conflict? How can I seek peace and unity in these areas?

Dear Friend,

You've just completed the first section of this challenge, and I am so proud of you for your dedication to clearing the path to peace in your life! Letting go of harmful attitudes and behaviors is not easy. Each day, you've faced the task of identifying the things that clutter your heart and keep you from fully experiencing God's presence. By releasing pride, dishonesty, anger, and other obstacles, you are making room for God's love and peace to fill every corner of your life.

Remember that clearing the path isn't a one-time process; it's a continual journey. As you continue, ask God to help you recognize anything else that needs to be released. With every step, you're drawing closer to Him and making space for His joy and purpose to flourish in your life.

Thank you for your courage and commitment. Keep moving forward, knowing that God is with you, cheering you on, and ready to fill your life with His peace.

With encouragement,
Your Sister In Christ

Days 8-16:
Clothing Yourself in Christ

(Putting On Godly Virtues)

Day 8: Put On Compassion

Scripture: "Be kind and compassionate to one another, forgiving each other, just as in Christ God forgave you." — **Ephesians 4:32**

Reflection Question: How can I show compassion today, even in small ways?

_____
_____
_____
_____
_____
_____
_____
_____
_____
_____
_____
_____
_____
_____
_____
_____
_____
_____
_____
_____

Day 9: Practice Kindness

Scripture: "Therefore, as God's chosen people, holy and dearly loved, clothe yourselves with kindness." — **Colossians 3:12**

Reflection Question: How can I be intentional in showing kindness to someone who might not expect it?

Day 10: Embrace Humility

Scripture: "Humble yourselves before the Lord, and he will lift you up." — **James 4:10**

Reflection Question: What does true humility look like in my life? Where can I put others first?

_____
_____
_____
_____
_____
_____
_____
_____
_____
_____
_____
_____
_____
_____
_____
_____
_____
_____
_____
_____

Day 11: Show Gentleness

Scripture: "Let your gentleness be evident to all. The Lord is near." — **Philippians 4:5**

Reflection Question: How can I respond with gentleness today, even in challenging situations?

Day 12: Cultivate Patience

Scripture: "Be completely humble and gentle; be patient, bearing with one another in love." — **Ephesians 4:2**

Reflection Question: Where am I quick to become impatient? How can waiting bring growth?

_____
_____
_____
_____
_____
_____
_____
_____
_____
_____
_____
_____
_____
_____
_____
_____
_____
_____
_____
_____
_____

Day 13: Pursue Forgiveness

Scripture: "Bear with each other and forgive one another… forgive as the Lord forgave you." — **Colossians 3:13**

Reflection Question: Is there someone I need to forgive or ask forgiveness from today?

Day 14: Radiate Love

Scripture: "And over all these virtues put on love, which binds them all together in perfect unity." — **Colossians 3:14**

Reflection Question: How can I show love to those around me today, especially in unexpected ways?

Day 15: Practice Self-Control

Scripture: "For the Spirit God gave us does not make us timid, but gives us power, love, and self-discipline." — **2 Timothy 1:7**

Reflection Question: In which area of my life do I need greater self-control?

Day 16: Extend Mercy

Scripture: "Blessed are the merciful, for they will be shown mercy." — **Matthew 5:7**

Reflection Question: How can I offer mercy to someone who has wronged or hurt me?

Dear Friend,

Congratulations on completing the second section of the challenge, "Clothing Yourself in Christ!" You have taken incredible steps to put on the virtues that reflect the character of Christ. Every act of kindness, humility, patience, and love you embraced this week has brought you closer to God and positively impacted those around you.

Remember that these virtues are not just ideals to admire—they are the qualities that God calls us to live out daily. By putting on these "garments of grace," you are living as a true reflection of His love. Let these qualities grow in your heart, and watch as they transform your relationships, outlook, and walk with God.

Thank you for clothing yourself in the qualities that matter most. Keep going, knowing that each act of kindness and love brings you closer to becoming the person God designed you to be.

In Christ's love,
Your Sister In Christ

Days 17-23:
Becoming a New Creature

(Embracing Your Identity in Christ)

Day 17: Renew Your Mind

Scripture: "Be transformed by the renewing of your mind." — **Romans 12:2**

Reflection Question: What thought patterns do I need to let go of? How can I align my thoughts with God's truth?

_____
_____
_____
_____
_____
_____
_____
_____
_____
_____
_____
_____
_____
_____
_____
_____
_____
_____
_____
_____
_____
_____

Day 18: Trust God's Work in You

Scripture: "Being confident of this, that he who began a good work in you will carry it on to completion." — **Philippians 1:6**

Reflection Question: Where do I need to trust God's work in my life, even if I can't see it yet?

Day 19: Walk in the Spirit

Scripture: "Since we live by the Spirit, let us keep in step with the Spirit." — **Galatians 5:25**

Reflection Question: How can I listen more closely to the Holy Spirit's guidance today?

Day 20: Embrace Your New Identity

Scripture: "If anyone is in Christ, the new creation has come: The old has gone, the new is here!" — **2 Corinthians 5:17**

Reflection Question: How does knowing I am a new creation in Christ impact the way I live?

Day 21: Rejoice in God's Grace

Scripture: "My grace is sufficient for you, for my power is made perfect in weakness." — **2 Corinthians 12:9**

Reflection Question: Where do I need to rely on God's grace rather than my own strength?

Day 22: Be Confident in Your Calling

Scripture: "For we are God's handiwork, created in Christ Jesus to do good works." — **Ephesians 2:10**

Reflection Question: What gifts or passions has God given me to serve others?

Day 23: Rest in God's Love

Scripture: "See what great love the Father has lavished on us, that we should be called children of God!" — **1 John 3:1**

Reflection Question: How can I remind myself daily of God's love and acceptance?

Dear Friend,

What an incredible milestone—you've completed this challenge's third section and taken the necessary steps toward embracing your identity as a new creation in Christ! Transformation isn't always easy; it requires us to let go of past patterns and mindsets that no longer serve us. But by putting off the old self and putting on the new, you are stepping into a life of purpose, freedom, and joy.

As you walk forward, remember that old habits or mistakes no longer define you. You are a beloved child of God, chosen, accepted, and renewed. This journey is about embracing your true identity in Christ and living out the purpose He has placed within you.

Keep moving forward in confidence, knowing that God is guiding you every step of the way. Embrace each day as a new opportunity to live in the freedom of your new identity in Christ.

With admiration and support,
Your Sister In Christ

Days 24-30:
Living the Transformation

(Practical Steps to Walk in Renewal)

Day 24: Reflect on the Day

Scripture: "Let us examine our ways and test them." — **Lamentations 3:40**

Reflection Question: How can I incorporate self-reflection daily to grow spiritually?

Day 25: Stay Rooted in Prayer

Scripture: "Devote yourselves to prayer, being watchful and thankful." — **Colossians 4:2**

Reflection Question: How can I deepen my prayer life as I walk in transformation?

Day 26: Meditate on Scripture

Scripture: "Keep this Book of the Law always on your lips; meditate on it day and night." — **Joshua 1:8**

Reflection Question: Which verses can I meditate on to focus on God's truth?

Day 27: Seek Accountability

Scripture: "As iron sharpens iron, so one person sharpens another." — **Proverbs 27:17**

Reflection Question: Who can I trust to encourage and hold me accountable on this journey?

Day 28: Serve Others Selflessly

Scripture: "Each of you should use whatever gift you have received to serve others." — **1 Peter 4:10**

Reflection Question: How can I serve someone selflessly today?

Day 29: Practice Gratitude

Scripture: "Give thanks in all circumstances; for this is God's will for you in Christ Jesus." — **1 Thessalonians 5:18**

Reflection Question: What can I be grateful for today, even in challenging situations?

Day 30: Live Out Your New Life

Scripture: "And whatever you do, whether in word or deed, do it all in the name of the Lord Jesus, giving thanks to God the Father through him." — **Colossians 3:17**

Reflection Question: How can I intentionally live each day in a way that reflects my new identity in Christ?

Congratulations! You Did It!

Congratulations on reaching Day 30 of this transformative journey! Today is all about celebrating how far you've come and committing to live out your renewed life with intention and purpose. You've let go of old habits and attitudes, embraced godly virtues, and discovered your identity as a new creation in Christ. Now, it's time to take all you've learned and put it into practice daily.

Living out your new life means reflecting Christ in everything you do—your words, actions, and choices. It means allowing the virtues you've put on to shape the way you interact with others, approach challenges, and navigate the ups and downs of life. Remember that transformation is an ongoing process. You are continually being renewed, strengthened, and guided by God's love and grace.

Commit to daily habits that will help sustain your transformation as you move forward. Keep spending time in prayer, meditating on God's Word, and surrounding yourself with people who encourage and support your journey. Let today be a fresh start to live fully in the freedom, love, and purpose that God has for you.

Call to Action:

Today, make a plan to live out your new life intentionally. Identify one way you can show God's love to others, one area where you can practice a new virtue, and one specific action that will keep you grounded in your faith journey. Take a moment to thank God for this journey and ask Him to guide you as you continue to walk in His truth.

My prayer is that you continue to walk in the truths you've discovered here. May you always remember that you are a new creation in Christ, deeply loved, and called to live a life of joy, love, and purpose. Keep this journey going beyond these 30 days. Let God's love guide you, transform you, and use you to be a light to others.

Well done, friend. Keep going strong, knowing that God has amazing things in store for you.

With love and congratulations,
Your Sister In Christ

Additional Resources:

Here is a list of additional books on transformation, spiritual growth, and living a Christ-centered life, with the Bible as the foundational and primary source:

1. **"The Bible"** (Primary Source)

    The Bible is the ultimate guide for spiritual transformation, offering God's wisdom, love, and instruction on how to live a life that reflects His character.

2. **"Celebration of Discipline: The Path to Spiritual Growth" by Richard J. Foster**

    This classic explores the spiritual disciplines that help Christians grow in their walk with God, covering practices such as prayer, fasting, study, and worship as pathways to deeper transformation.

3. **"The Pursuit of Holiness" by Jerry Bridges**

    Bridges examines what it means to live a holy life and how to practically pursue holiness by relying on God's grace, addressing both the human effort and divine power involved in our transformation.

4. **"Renovation of the Heart: Putting on the Character of Christ" by Dallas Willard**

    This book comprehensively examines inner transformation, showing how our thoughts, emotions, and behaviors must be renewed to truly reflect Christ's heart.

5. **"The Purpose Driven Life: What on Earth Am I Here For?" by Rick Warren**

    Warren's book provides practical insights on living a purpose-centered life, helping readers understand God's purpose for them and offering steps to deepen their walk with Him.

6. **"Emotionally Healthy Spirituality: It's Impossible to Be Spiritually Mature While Remaining Emotionally Immature" by Peter Scazzero**

    Scazzero teaches how emotional health and spiritual maturity are intertwined and offers ways to address emotional barriers that prevent us from growing spiritually.

7. **"Mere Christianity" by C.S. Lewis**

    This powerful exploration of Christian beliefs includes insights into how God transforms us through faith, emphasizing personal renewal and the importance of living as a new creation in Christ.

8. "The Practice of the Presence of God" by Brother Lawrence

A timeless classic that encourages believers to experience God's presence in every moment of daily life, offering wisdom on how to live with a heart fully devoted to God.

9. "The Pursuit of God" by A.W. Tozer

Tozer's book explores the deep longing to know God more intimately and encourages readers to continually live with a passion for constantly experiencing His presence.

10. "Spiritual Disciplines for the Christian Life" by Donald S. Whitney

Whitney offers practical advice on practicing spiritual disciplines, such as prayer, worship, and Bible study, to help readers grow in godliness and draw closer to God.

11. "Living the Spirit-Formed Life" by Jack Hayford

Hayford outlines foundational principles for a Spirit-led life, including personal transformation through disciplines like worship, meditation, and humility.

12. **"Transformed by God's Grace: Spiritual Renewal in the Christian Life" by J.I. Packer**

    This book examines the role of God's grace in transforming the believer, discussing how grace shapes our lives and character to become more like Christ.

13. **"Becoming a Woman of Excellence" by Cynthia Heald** (for women)

    Heald encourages women to pursue godly character, inner transformation, and excellence in all areas of life through biblical principles.

14. **"The Hole in Our Holiness: Filling the Gap Between Gospel Passion and the Pursuit of Godliness" by Kevin DeYoung**

    This book challenges believers to pursue holiness in their everyday lives and demonstrates how holiness is central to our identity in Christ.

15. **"How People Grow: What the Bible Reveals About Personal Growth" by Dr. Henry Cloud and Dr. John Townsend**

    Cloud and Townsend delve into biblical principles of growth and transformation, addressing how relationships, boundaries, and healing affect our spiritual journey.

In conjunction with the Bible, these books offer valuable insights and practical tools to support a life of spiritual growth, transformation, and deeper intimacy with God.

Meet the Author:
Alisa Ladawn Grace

Alisa Ladawn Grace is a woman devoted to faith, service, and guiding others toward meaningful transformation. As a retired school administrator, Transformation Life Coach, author, and dedicated local missionary, Alisa has spent over 30 years inspiring individuals to embrace God's love, grow in faith, and live purposefully. Her unwavering belief in the power of God's transformative love is evident in every aspect of her life and work.

With a specialist degree in curriculum and instruction, Alisa has significantly impacted students, educators, and families, helping them unlock their potential academically and spiritually. As a Transformation Life Coach, she continues to empower individuals to align their lives with God's purpose through intentional living and heart transformation.

Alisa's latest book, *Renewed: The Transformational Power of Putting Off the Old and Putting On the New*, is a profound guide to true spiritual renewal. In this work, she helps readers identify the behaviors and attitudes God calls us to "put off" and embrace the virtues He desires us to "put on," such as humility, compassion, and love. Through relatable stories, practical steps, and reflection questions, Alisa offers a pathway for readers to draw closer to God, live as new creations in Christ, and experience lasting peace and purpose.

Her passion for personal and spiritual growth is also reflected in her previous works, including *Mind Architect: How Your Thoughts Design Your Destiny*, where she explores the connection between mindset and reality, equipping readers with tools to break free from limiting beliefs and design a purposeful, God-aligned life. In her children's books and curriculum, she fosters a sense of civic engagement, faith, and good habits in young minds.

Through her writing, coaching, and ministry, Alisa Ladawn Grace continues to be a guiding light, inspiring readers to embrace transformation, deepen their connection with God, and live out His purpose with renewed faith and intentionality.

www.ingramcontent.com/pod-product-compliance
Lightning Source LLC
Chambersburg PA
CBHW070207100426
42743CB00013B/3089